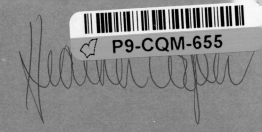

CARNAVAL PERPETUEL

For my daughter Sarah
If only everything I started
could turn out as well.

◆

Copyright © 1987 by Heather Cooper

All rights reserved in all countries. No part
of this publication may be reproduced or
transmitted in any form or by any electronic
or mechanical means including information
storage and retrieval system without permis-
sion from the publisher except by a reviewer
who may quote brief passages in a review.

Published by
Le Carnaval Perpétuel
Heather Cooper Communication
By Design Ltd.
2 Gloucester Street, Suite 302
Toronto, Ontario
Canada M4Y 1L5
Printed in Canada

ISBN 0-920668-44-5

CARNAVAL PERPETUEL

Le Carnaval Perpétuel

Life is a continuum of theatre,
A character which never shewes a face;
For when its masque at last is strip'd away
Another masque is lhere to take its place.

◆

Heather Cooper is a Canadian artist who
believes in life as 'le carnaval perpétuel';
"We get wrapped up – sometimes torn up –
by a moment in life because each of us is a
certain kind of person in a certain kind of
mask. We sometimes forget there are other
layers below, and how helpful it can be to
peel away the surface mask and see what the
person beneath it has to offer."

In her art, her commercial illustrations and
her package design, Heather Cooper believes
that the most powerful communication,
whether it's between an artist and a viewer
or a business and a customer, hits home by
penetrating all the layers, all of the masks,
and breaks through all the barriers at once.

A collection of works by
HEATHER COOPER

Published by Le Carnaval Perpétuel
Toronto, Canada 1987

Years ago, my father and mother made me a gift of a wonderful wooden box. The hinges were brass. The handle was leather. And the initials glued to the front panel were mine.

When I opened the box I discovered a neat row of oil paints in colorful tubes, glass bottles with turpentine and linseed oil, a pair of canvases and a handful of long-handled brushes – longer than my canvases were wide.

It was my eighth birthday.

I began to paint for love and quickly became a passionate consumer of cardboard-backed canvas boards. The loving gift of my parents had awakened a gift inside me.
I responded with one of my own: my first painting, an imaginary cottage in an orchard.

My childhood accomplishments were given freely to relatives and friends to decorate their homes. In return, they gave me encouragement and confidence.

The circle was complete, with the gift returning to the giver.

I soon learned that my creative efforts could also be exchanged for money. It was a timely discovery since, for growing teenagers, life is an endless list of needs: records, red T-strap shoes, money to spend with friends. I could satisfy these needs by selling my paintings.

I knew I was onto something good here. But this early financial success brought with it something I hadn't experienced before: an occasional feeling of detachment from my work. It was a feeling that would surface from time to time throughout my career.

From the age of fourteen I knew what that career would be. At eighteen, with a decade of 'experience' under my belt and a mixed bag of samples under my arm, I went off to look for

work. My first full-time job was with a company I'd found in the Yellow Pages. All I knew at the time was that they did some kind of art there. I wasn't sure what it was or what I would do there. For that matter, neither were they.

Over the years I worked hard at my commercial art. I learned to accept art as a commodity and became more and more successful at creating it. But for all of the comforts and rewards of the materialistic world, my greatest satisfactions always emerged from the work I created for love.

The sense of detachment that had surfaced first in my early teens now became more sharply defined. The professional artist, I learned, must live with the dualistic roles of idealist and realist.

The quandary of dualism rears its head many times and in many ways during an artist's development.
To gain experience and insight – not to mention the clients who keep you in business – an artist must be outgoing and worldly. Yet finding the time required to create, demands a lifestyle that borders on monastic.

An artist's talent, inspiration and imagination are not a commodity, but a gift. And the vitality of that gift is reflected in the work. The art that we have come to treasure most is that which transmits enough of this vitality to revive our souls. An artist whose work touches us earns our gratitude by establishing a bond that enriches us all.

But the introduction of a fee cuts the circle of giving, and severs the ties of gratitude. When a market value has to be determined, art must suddenly be placed on a scale and compared with other art. Those responsible for this process of evaluation must distance themselves from the item that's being priced, and this distance inhibits the creation of bonds.

Therein lies the artist's dilemma.

How can someone who has chosen to labor with a gift survive in a society whose commerce consists almost exclusively of the buying and selling of commodities? Accept a commission of a commercial nature and the evaluation of the work has taken place already. The artist has become a number on a cost benefit analysis sheet, which weighs the fee against potential profits.

Today's artists work within the financial boundaries set by the market and the good ones become financially successful. But how much of what they do transmits the artist's true vitality?

The greatest works of commercial art are never properly rewarded and likely never will be. This is because in order to achieve that greatness the artist leaps beyond the commercial boundaries, and applies talent and imagination that far exceed everyone's original expectations.

Only by giving from the heart in this way will an artist summon the inspiration, ideas and insight that kindle the finest work.

When our gift mind loses out to our money mind the less fulfilled we become, as artists, as individuals and as a society.

The solution, I believe, is to seek out those assignments that allow a good balance between creative inspiration and commercial incentive.

On the following pages are projects that strike this balance for me, assignments that not only filled a communications need but also provided the opportunity for me to give something from the heart.

In any walk of life, no man is an island. It often takes the collaboration of other professionals to bring an idea to life. Over the years, I've been fortunate in working with some of the finest people in the business; my work and my life have been the richer for it.

Ten years ago, in a moment of clouded vision, I threw out my old paint box. It was old and outgrown and soiled by the smudges of childhood. After it was gone, I thought about it often.

Recently, I celebrated my 40th birthday and a close friend gave me a wonderful gift: my old paint box. He had seen me discard it and rescued it without my knowing. It was returned to me all cleaned and polished and warm with memories.

I shall never throw it away again.

Heather Cooper

Curtain Up: It's a curious fact of life that in North America the greatest supporters of the performing arts are neither philanthropists, nor governments, nor the paying audience – but the artists themselves. With a handful of star-studded exceptions, local performers live a precarious existence; the average wage is insufficient to keep even a small family above the poverty line.

Small wonder that community arts organizations are rarely able to promote themselves with big budget campaigns.

Hence the revival of the poster. A poster can promote an event in a way that is striking, tasteful, and affordable. In addition to promoting a specific series of performances, posters can be sold in theater souvenir shops to help raise funds. Good posters also have a timeless quality that makes them effective "billboards" for performing groups for years to come.

Contrary to what some may think, designing a poster is not easy work. Far from it. It's a challenge to turn out what is essentially a piece of advertising in a way that will appeal to the fickle fashion-sense of trendy urban buyers, yet still be on their walls a dozen years later.

Nor is it always easy to deal with performers, past and present. The nature of their work often demands that they be blessed with an ego at least as large as that of the artist! And to do a good job, the artist has to steal a little of their limelight.

Sometimes the poster theme is an embellishment of an existing idea. Occasionally, the central image becomes an icon, or graphic trademark, of the company itself. My 1977 painting for the Canadian Opera Company remains a key part of their public imagery more than a decade later.

This is perhaps the most satisfying part of creating posters for the

arts. When a graphic depiction of a performance, a book or a musical score really succeeds, it achieves its own public recognition and travels through time as part – and partner – of the work that inspired it.

Above: Graphic identity for Hendry Arts Inc., consultants, organizers, and producers.

Below: Graphic identity for Ra, a theater production with performances running from dusk to dawn.

Facing page: Canadian Opera Company, oil on canvas, 18 by 24 in. Commissioned in 1977 for an edition of posters. Private collection.

Page 10: Bluebeards's Egg, oil on canvas, 16 by 20 in. Commissioned by Canadian author Margaret Atwood for an edition of posters and a book jacket. Authors don't usually get this involved with their covers; it was a brave move that took a good part of her publisher's advance. Private collection.

Page 11: A Flight of Fantasy, oil on canvas, 21 by 23 in. Commissioned by The National Ballet of Canada, 1978, for an edition of posters. Private collection.

Page 12: The Muses, oil on canvas, 17 by 20½ in. Commissioned by The Financial Post as a poster and program cover promoting the link between business and the arts, 1985. Private collection.

Page 13: Stravinsky, oil on canvas, 17 by 20½ in. Commissioned in 1979 by composer/ musician Paul Hoffert as an album cover and poster. Paul bought the original painting for his collection and, as a joke, paid me for it in 5,000 one-dollar bills! I kept the money in a suitcase under my bed for three months before I worked up enough nerve to take it to the bank.

Page 14: Athene, oil on canvas, 18 by 24 in. Commissioned by the Newspaper Advertising Bureau, 1984, as a poster and cover for a newspaper section. Athene was the goddess of the useful arts whose skills as a weaver were once challenged by a mere mortal. Athene responded by weaving the wings of the butterfly; when the mortal, Arachne, turned out to be a sore loser, Athene turned her into a spider. The ribbons in Athene's hand represent the primary colors of contemporary newspaper printing. Private collection.

Pages 15, 16 and 17: Magicians, oil on canvas, 20 by 24 in. Commissioned by the Festival of Festivals, 1985, for an edition of posters. As this is North America's premier film festival, I presented film as the ultimate magic. Out of the little black box comes movement, color, and luminosity, symbolized here by the butterflies. The robes are also made up of patterns from butterfly wings. Private collection.

Page 18: Macbeth, oil on board, 5¼ by 5¾ in., began in 1985 for a series of booklets based on Shakespeare's plays, a project that didn't materialize.

Page 19: Queen of Spades, oil on canvas, 12½ by 22½ in. Commissioned by the Philadelphia Opera Company and the Ford Byrne Agency, 1984, for a limited edition of prints and posters. Cigna Corporation Collection.

Pages 20 and 21: The Houston Opera, oil on canvas, 24 by 18 in. Commissioned in 1986 by Ogilvy and Mather, Houston, Texas, for an edition of posters and a publication insert. Private collection.

Page 22: Guardian of Treasures, oil on canvas, 15¾ by 24 in. Commissioned by the Joseph Meyerhoff Symphony Hall, Baltimore, for an edition of posters and a program cover. Private collection.

CANADIAN OPERA 1977

DON CARLOS ✦ THE MAGIC FLUTE
DAUGHTER OF THE REGIMENT ✦ WOZZECK

O'KEEFE CENTRE, TORONTO, SEPTEMBER 14TH TO OCTOBER 29TH

THE FINANCIAL POST
BUSINESS IN THE ARTS AWARDS
VANCOUVER 1985

L'HISTOIRE DU SOLDAT

IGOR STRAVINSKY

CONCERTO FOR CONTEMPORARY VIOLIN

PAUL HOFFERT

AUL HOFFERT, CONDUCTOR   STEVEN STARYK, VIOLIN

FESTIVAL *of* FESTIVALS

SEPTEMBER 5-14, 1985

Toronto Ontario Canada

Merrily, merrily whirled the wheels of
    the dizzying dances
Under the orchard-trees and down
    the path to the meadows;
Old folk and young together, and
    children mingled among them.
Henry Wadsworth Longfellow (1807-1882)
Evangeline

In 1984, the City of Toronto celebrated its 150th birthday with a
month-long party, the first of its kind
in North America. The Toronto International Festival brought together
groups as diverse as the Hamburg
Ballet, the Dance Theater of Harlem,
India's Kathakali Dance Drama, and
the Mormon Tabernacle Choir – in
250 different performances right
through the month of June.

As with any new venture using public
funds, this Festival also attracted its
share of critics. Back in the planning
stages some members of city council
objected to the travel expenses of the
Festival's globe-trotting organizers.
Others, ignoring the fact that dozens
of events would be priced at $5 a
seat and that many others would be
free, objected to the $90 admission
charge for the Metropolitan Opera.
When it came to promoting the
Festival, it was very important to
present it as a party that promised a
good time for everyone, regardless
of income.

So, in designing the graphic identity
I wanted a symbol that would not
only represent song and dance, but
also suggest a spirit of lighthearted
fun. Central to the visual theme was
a little character who is part Pan,
part satyr. Both of these mythical
creatures are well known for their
libido. I felt that this was an appropriate choice as I have always seen
dance in a very earthy light.

The Pan appeared on three-
dimensional displays, street banners,
and on every other item that the
Festival produced, including posters,
brochures, T-shirts, programs, signs,
and even satchels.

TORONTO INTERNATIONAL ✤FESTIVAL✤

A ONCE IN A LIFETIME GALA CELEBRATION OF MUSIC & DANCE

Above and below: Graphic identity for the Toronto International Festival.

Page 24: The promotional poster, oil on board, 24 by 32½ in. I introduced the ribbons to add to the feeling of celebration and activity.

Page 25: Toronto International Festival street banner. These colorful streamers helped to create a carnival-like atmosphere for the city.

Pages 26 and 27: The Twilight Series, celebrating the folk singers and street musicians who delighted audiences of the Toronto International Festival with their free evening concerts. One of six limited-edition silk screens for posters and fine art prints. Each of the prints depicted a performing troupe. Strung together, they created a procession led by Pan. Pen and ink, 15½ by 22½ in. Black and metallic gold.

Pages 28 and 29: Death in Venice, by the Canadian Opera Company. Although the Festival was international in every sense, almost 80 percent of the performers were Canadians. Pen and ink, 15½ by 22½ in. One of six limited-edition silk screens for posters and fine art prints. Black and metallic gold.

When the final curtain came down,
Festival director Muriel Sherrin, and
Judith Hendry, director of marketing
and communications, and all of the
other organizers enjoyed the last
laugh over their critics. By month's
end, some 300,000 people had turned
out to enjoy the work of more than
12,600 performers, in such diverse
locations as Maple Leaf Gardens,
Deer Park United Church, public
parks, and city sidewalks. And when
the final figures were tallied, the
Toronto International Festival had
made a profit of $100,000, which
went into an endowment fund for
the arts.

A ONCE IN A LIFETIME GALA
CELEBRATION OF MUSIC & DANCE

TORONTO
INTERNATIONAL
FESTIVAL

JUNE 1·30·1984·TORONTO·ONTARIO·CANADA

Stratford, Ontario, like its English namesake, is famous for its parklands, the Avon River, and a long love affair with William Shakespeare. The Stratford Festival draws about half a million theater enthusiasts each year, almost a third of them from the United States.

Since it opened in 1953, the Stratford Festival has given young Canadian talent an opportunity to learn from the best by sharing the stage with some of the world's greatest actors, who make regular appearances here. Today, the Festival is regarded as North America's leading classical theater. In addition to Shakespeare, it offers a great range of entertainment, from serious works by serious young playwrights to the rollicking comic operas of Gilbert and Sullivan.

For an artist, working with the Festival can be an exciting time, full of emotional turmoil. At times, the in-fighting and backstage maneuvering has reached epic proportions, with conflict enough to inspire a drama of its own. But on the positive side, an artist will find ample grist for the cerebral mill in the lavish visual content and intellectual inspiration of the productions. For more impetus there is – all politics aside – a continuing drive to make each season's performances more successful than those of the year before.

It's always satisfying to work for people who know what they want. But it isn't always easy. A further challenge in illustrating promotional pieces for a Stratford production is that, at the time the work is commissioned, there is precious little physical material to draw from. This necessitates working closely with the artistic director to extract an idea of the look and the "feel" of the production. As well, I always spend a lot of time with the plays themselves, learning the idiosyncrasies of the more important characters.

Using the imagination to symbolize a work of imagination: what more could an artist ask for?

Above: Most of my work for Stratford came in the early 1980s. This commemorative mark celebrated the Festival's 30th birthday in 1982.

Below: Graphic identity for the Stratford Festival, 1982.

Page 31: The Mikado, *oil on canvas, 18 by 24 in. Commissioned in 1982 for an edition of posters and promotional items. Private collection.*

Page 32: Shakespeare the Gardener, *oil on board, 18 by 24 in. Commissioned in 1983 for an edition of posters and promotional items. Although we tend to regard him as a sophisticated urban gentleman, Shakespeare was a country man who loved the outdoors. (This was the side of him that I wanted to show in this painting.) Private collection.*

Page 33: Shakespeare, *oil on canvas, 15¾ by 19 in. Commissioned in 1982 for an edition of posters. The Hirsch Collection.*

Pages 34 and 35: Gilbert & Sullivan, *oil on canvas, 18 by 24 in. Commissioned in 1984 for an edition of posters. Private collection.*

Pages 36 and 37: W. S. Gilbert based even his wildest story lines on fact. The Gondoliers has its roots in 15th-Century Venice, where an ardent Republican was appointed king and invited all his friends to form a royal court. The message is neatly summed up in Gilbert's words: "When everyone is somebodee, then no one's anybody!" Oil on canvas, 18 by 20 in. Commissioned in 1983 for an edition of prints. Private collection.

THE MIKADO

BY GILBERT & SULLIVAN

JUNE 7 - AUGUST 1, 1982   AVON THEATRE

STRATFORD FESTIVAL CANADA

STRATFORD
FESTIVAL

THE GONDOLIERS

BY GILBERT & SULLIVAN

JUNE 6 ~ JULY 31, 1983 STRATFORD FESTIVAL CANADA AVON THEATRE

ARTISTIC DIRECTOR JOHN HIRSCH

When my clients, Kim and Marjorie Ironmonger, returned from a trip to England with the idea of opening a salon for bridal and formal wear they asked me to develop a name. Their gowns were to be created by an English designer who worked with fine silks and wonderfully intricate laces. The style would be romantic and traditional, hinting at the realm of Guinevere, Wuthering Heights, and the English country garden of the 17th Century.

In this age of drip-dry clothing, someone would be creating gowns that would inevitably become heirlooms, handed down from mother to daughter.

To find a suitable identity, I delved into the history of lace and discovered there a fascinating world. The more I learned, the more amazed I became that lace had even survived to the present day.

From the Middle Ages on, it had to stand up against "sumptuary laws", those curious edicts that dictated how much one could spend on clothing. In 12th-Century France, for example, only the "lady of the manor" was allowed to buy more than two dresses a year. And in England, under Henry VIII, no one below the rank of knight was permitted to wear clothing trimmed with lace. Other monarchs passed similar laws on the grounds that lace was far too good to waste on the common people. But the common people had ideas of their own: one popular tradition was the wearing of a cheaper lace to the country fairs held on St. Audrey's Day (October 17). In time, the name St. Audrey contracted into "tawdry", a word that still means something "showy", or of little value.

For the name that I wanted I went to the opposite side of the economic scale and found Valenciennes, a Flemish town famed for its lace through the 1700s. The standards

Valencienne

Above: Valencienne wordmark. The ornamental bouquet suggests the light and frothy nature of the gowns, with their laces, flounces, and embroidery.

Below: Detail from a series of ornamental embellishments.

Facing page: (Above) The Valencienne press kit was presented to media people with a nosegay of real flowers enclosed in a lace ruffle.

(Below) The company's stationery, along with the lace-covered potpourri, a gift for potential clients.

Pages 40 and 41: Portraits of a Wedding, magazine advertisements, photographed by Tim Saunders.

Page 42: The Royal Gown, exhibit promotion and magazine advertisement, designed by Andrea Wilkins at the request of Sarah Ferguson on her engagement to HRH the Duke of York. Although this gown was not the one selected for the Royal Wedding, the awe-inspiring craftsmanship encouraged the owners of Valencienne to buy it and bring it to North America.

Page 43: Valencienne Perfume.

here were so exacting that even the most skilled workers – usually young girls with keen eyes and soft, uncalloused hands – were able to turn out less than two inches of lace a day!

That image of painstaking detail, and the pleasing sound of the word "Valenciennes" seemed right for a new retail business. We simply shortened the name to "Valencienne".

In all of the promotional graphics, I tried to set the stage and to create a mood of fantasy, drawing inspiration from the intricate design of the gowns themselves.

Tim Saunders, one of Canada's renowned photographers, turned Valencienne's magazine advertisements into works of art with his tenderness of lighting and sensitivity of arrangement.

The 'Theme' Wedding.

A Mid-Summer Dream.

Valencienne

Valencienne

Appointment

_____

_____

Bridal Design
21-25 Bloor Street West
Toronto, Ontario
Canada M4W 1A3
(416) 962-8558

Valencienne

Bridal Design
21-25 Bloor Street West
Toronto, Ontario
Canada M4W 1A3
(416) 962-8558

Valencienne

Portrait of a Wedding

✦✦ Two Small Friends of the Bride ✦✦
By appointment, you may see our *complete bridal collection*,
at *Valencienne* 21-25 Bloor Street West, Toronto • (416) 962-8558

Valencienne

Portrait of a Wedding

⇘ A Small Friend of the Bride ⇘

By appointment, you may see our *complete bridal collection,*
at *Valencienne* 21-25 Bloor Street West, Toronto • (416) 962-8558

Anyone who grew up in Toronto during the 1950s, as I did, has seen the city go through some remarkable changes. From its well-earned postwar image as a frumpy, abstemious, largely WASPish community, Toronto has blossomed into a good-looking, cosmopolitan, fun-loving city of 2 million, with a downtown core that still manages to be clean and safe and respectful of its past.

The story of the Elmwood is typical of the spirit that has turned Toronto into "a city that works". The Elmwood was built almost a hundred years ago as Canada's first YWCA residence. Today, it's an elegant women's club, spa, restaurant, and bar. The original red brick facade of the building has been restored and given a matching brick and glass extension.

Behind all the changes are two remarkable Toronto women: Sherry Brydson, who looked after the business end, and Barbara Elson, who specialized in the space planning and interior design.

Their aim was to provide a tasteful yet friendly retreat, where executive and professional women could steal away from the pressures of business. The Elmwood Women's Club, which occupies the upper three floors of the building, was the soul of the new enterprise. The other facilities would be open to the general public.

The Bangkok Garden Restaurant was the brainchild of Sherry Brydson, who has spent a lot of time in Thailand and has become greatly attached to its traditions and its food. The love affair is reflected in her hands-on management of the restaurant.

I was asked to develop graphic identities for each of the building's components: women's club, spa, restaurant, and bar. I was given a free hand except for one little wrinkle – a small triangular motif that was taken from the Thai

decorative arts. Whatever I did with the various identities would have to include this motif.

Middle Column: (Above) Graphic identifier for the women's club.

(Center) Graphic identifier for the Bangkok Garden restaurant.

(Below) The Brass Flamingo is the name of the bar, which has a large brass flamingo as part of its decor. Naturally, it became a key part of the logo.

Facing page: To promote the Elmwood Women's Club, I designed a brochure that opened out into a poster, showing the facilities of the club. Also included was a pen and ink drawing of the building, from which this detail was taken.

Page 46: (Above) Wordmark for The Spa at the Elmwood.

(Below) Envie, a line of creams and body lotions formulated by the Elmwood's founders and offered for sale at the spa.

Page 47: A variety of paper products were designed to enhance the Envie line and strengthen the image of the spa itself.

The Spa
at the
Elmwood

EnVie
Splash
Tonique
110 ml

EnVie
Moisturiser
Hydratant
110 ml

EnVie
Body Treat
Soins du corps
110 ml

EnVie
Cleanser
Nettoyant
110 ml

EnVie

Moisturiser
Hydratant
110 ml

The Spa
at the
Elmwood

The Spa
at the
Elmwood

EnVie

In 1980 I signed an agreement with a Chicago company, Ruby Street, to design a series of cards, wrapping paper, gift boxes, and stationery, which they would manufacture and distribute under the Heather Cooper designer name.

My idea was to develop a series of designs that related to each other: the border on the card, for instance, would match the border on the paper. Each series of designs would work together in compatible color ranges.

What I didn't realize at the time was that the only way that I was ever going to make the concept work was to first buy a chain of stores. Tradition seems to dictate that greeting cards be displayed in one place, gift boxes three aisles over, and the gift wrap somewhere between shaving cream and sporting goods – miles from where you'd reasonably expect to find it. Our distributors were either unable or unwilling to persuade retailers to display the components of our lines in one place. I always felt that if I could go into the store and demonstrate its potential, the idea could be made to work. But I was in Canada, and 90 percent of the retailers were in the United States.

Despite that frustration, these lines sold very well, except for the stationery, which had to be priced higher than most people were willing to pay.

But as sales of my greeting cards, gift wrap, and gift boxes continued to grow, I couldn't help thinking that I was onto a good thing. True, there were clashes along the way, such as the one inspired by the Valentine that showed a girl's bottom in the shape of a heart and fringed with lace. The distributors rejected it as obscene. A minor annoyance but it rankled.

Still, I reasoned that once I had three or four series going, it would mean that work that I had produced two or three years ago would continue to generate an income.

Above and below: Cards from the autumn line.

Facing Page: Papers from the autumn line; papers and card from the flower line.

Pages 50 and 51: Valentine cards and gift wrap.

Pages 52 and 53: Early American gift wrap.

Pages 54, 55, 56 and 57: Cards and gift wrap from the Oriental line.

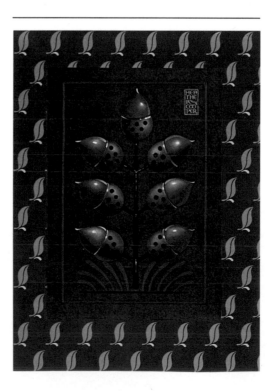

Unfortunately, that wasn't the case. When I sat down and weighed the earnings against what I was still putting into the project just to keep the line current, I found that I was barely breaking even. In hindsight, I was wrong to put this kind of effort into such low-ticket items. You have to sell a lot of wrapping paper at $1.50 to $2.00 before you can recoup the costs of manufacturing, distributing, and retailing, and you have to do all that before you begin to make money for yourself.

Anyone considering a similar venture should begin by producing a book on a particular subject. From the book, the same color art and separations could then be used to produce a calendar, then used again to produce the cards and gift wrap. If the book breaks even, most of your design time has already been paid for, and whatever you clear on the rest is gravy.

I hope someone tries it, because I'm a great believer in the entrepreneurial artist. Most of us have faith in our artistic skills but lack confidence in our business judgment.

In the case of the Valentine's "obscenity", my judgment proved to be right three years later when the distributors approached me about it again. This time, they not only wanted the card with the girl's bottom – they wanted a whole series designed around it!

I took some pleasure in giving them, appropriately enough, the bum's rush.

I have always tried to take time to produce work for myself. In the early part of my career, before I established some sort of reputation, I wasn't given a lot of freedom on the job; so the opportunities for self-expression weren't the same as they are today. That made it important to have some kind of outlet for my innermost feelings; and working for myself provided it.

Personal work releases personal emotions, some of which run very deep. What emerges on the canvas are ideas that no one is ever likely to pay you to express. Yet these ideas are part of what makes the complete artist, part of the well from which we draw inspiration for everything we do, commercial work included.

As the years pass, confidence grows and one's reputation solidifies. Then it becomes appropriate – even desirable – to bring more of the inner self to commercial projects.

And herein lies a trap. For the more that one is allowed to contribute from the heart, the greater the emotional entanglement. It becomes difficult – often impossible – to regard such work as something that is being done for money. The result can be an expenditure of time out of all proportion to the negotiated fee. That's good for the heart and soul – and every other corner that the artist in you rules. But it can be a problem for the part of you that has to pay the bills.

It can also lead you to question your own judgment when you're working evenings, Saturdays, and Sundays for weeks on end and still have very little financial reward. Perhaps that's the price of remaining an artist first and a business person second. If so, it's a price I'm happy to pay.

A far more serious drawback to putting so much of yourself into commercial work is that it reduces the need to keep creating paintings on your own. If too much personal

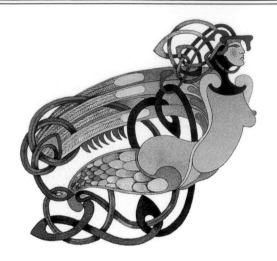

satisfaction is drawn from corporate assignments, long periods of time may pass before you return to doing anything for yourself. Personal ideas begin to accumulate, and remain unfulfilled; you persuade yourself that you'll get to them sooner or later. But as you continue to grow, new ideas replace them in importance. The earlier ones fall away before you've had a chance to do anything about them. The tragedy comes in knowing that you've let a moment in time slip between your fingers.

At this stage in my life I feel a need to express my feelings free and clear, with no encumberances and no one else to please. That doesn't mean vanishing from society to work in isolation and to exhibit the results in galleries. But it does mean setting aside more time away from business to devote to personal creativity.

Some of the images on these pages found their way into commercial applications. But that wasn't why they were created. All these works began as paintings for myself. Perhaps that's why they rank among my favorites.

Middle Column: (Above) The Figurehead, 1980, watercolor on paper, 4 by 5 in. This image was later used on stationery for Phoenician Explorations, a group engaged in the financing of searches for sunken treasure. Private collection.

(Below) The Bird, 1980, watercolor on paper, 6 by 8 in. One of 16 images portraying the mythology of the sea. Private collection.

Facing Page: Marilyn Lightstone, 1973, oil on canvas, 24 by 72 in. Collection of Moses Znaimer.

Page 60: Sarah and the Zebra, 1976, oil on canvas, 24 by 24 in. Artist's collection. This painting appeared as the cover of a book, The Illustrated Child, and as an anti-smoking poster. Sarah is my daughter.

Page 61: The Lion and the Lamb, 1975, oil on board, 13 by 15 in. I painted this work to convey the dilemma of a woman in business. How am I perceived, lion or lamb? Later, I found that this dilemma was shared, not just by people but by corporations. The image became the cover of a promotional booklet. Private collection.

Page 62: Simi, 1974, oil on canvas, 24 by 28 in. Private collection.

Page 63: The Cats, 1970, oil on canvas, 48 by 48 ins. Private collection.

Pages 64 and 65: Sarah and Pierrot, 1986, oil on canvas, 22 by 33 in. Featured on a promotional poster for Scollard Films. Left page shows detail.

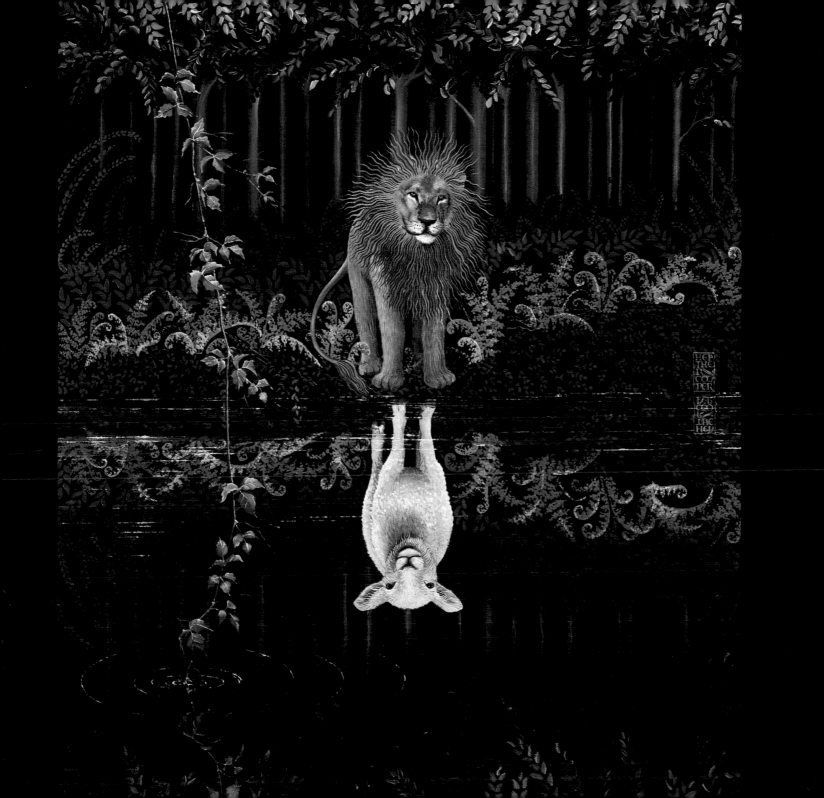

Occasionally I run into people who ask, "What do you do?" and expect a one-word answer. In this age of specialization, some of us have trouble accepting that one person can be a graphic designer, illustrator, and marketing person all in one. But my relationship with Yardley in the late 1970s allowed me to wear all three hats at once.

Yardley at the time was losing business. Its image, which had been so strong during the Carnaby St. bloom of the 1960s, was fading quickly. Many of its products were sadly out of date.

The company first approached me to make minor changes to its packaging. I didn't think that would do a thing to help and said so, not expecting to hear from them again. But a short time later they called and asked me to come and tell them more. That meeting would result in one of the most bittersweet assignments of my career.

To make the extreme kind of changes that were needed at Yardley would take the full cooperation of senior management. We were given even more than that: the key executives, who were all new to their posts, became productive members of our redevelopment team. Nights and weekends, day in and day out, I worked with Bob Demers, the president, Ildiko Evans-Marshall, the marketing director, and Conrad Heiby, who was in charge of production.

Up to then, Yardley products had been sold both from pegboards and cosmetic counters. We decided to focus our efforts on pegboards, which better suited the image and pricing structure of the products.

This was where I made an interesting discovery. Placing the product inside the blister pack on the back of the cardboard instead of on the front would tip the weight so that the pack-

age faced up toward the customer. The advantage to that seems so obvious today, but at the time almost all blister packs were weighted to the front, which tipped the face down and away.

In addition to redesigning all the packages, we created a store unit that held the packages and allowed the customer to experiment with different colors. This increased Yardley's impact in the store and strengthened its involvement with customers. Other promotions included banners, posters, gift boxes, and little booklets that hung from the pegs.

The end result was a sharp increase in sales for Yardley. But what none of us knew at the time was that the company's owners, British American Tobacco, intended to sell Yardley off.

In their wisdom, they sold it not as one complete unit but broke it up into components and sold each part separately. Everything we did soon disappeared.

Ten years later I still regard that decision as one of the heartbreaks of my life.

Middle Column: (Above) Yardley wordmark. The company was almost 200 years old, which some saw as a drawback in a fashion-conscious industry. We turned age into an advantage by conveying a sense of tradition.

(Below) A color guide helped each customer to choose the most suitable shade for her complexion and hair color.

Facing page: Yardley cosmetic packaging.

Page 68: A Mon Seul Désir, detail from a reproduction of a 16th-Century tapestry chosen as a promotional image for its highly romantic content.

Page 69: Gift box and promotional booklet bearing the tapestry theme.

Page 70: Classical Woman, oil on canvas, 18¼ by 25¼ in. Commissioned for application in promotional items. Private collection.

Page 71: Pages from the Yardley promotional booklet.

Pages 72 and 73: Woodland Sorcery, photographic still life by Canadian photographer Bob Wiginton, created to promote a color range.

Page 74: A winding pattern for Lotus.

Page 75: Roses and Lotus packaging for bath salts, talcum powder, and soaps.

Page 76: (Above) Lavender packaging for bath salts, talcum powder, and soaps.

(Below) Gift box: a tin fashioned after an historic Yardley product.

Page 77: Wooden gift boxes.

Pages 78 and 79: Lemonwood and Sea Mist soap packaging.

Pages 80 and 81: Sea Shells. I've saved shells for years and the design of the Sea Mist packaging gave me the opportunity and the motivation to expand my collection. Later, I removed the shells one by one from their white background, re-glued them onto black, and had a coffee table built around the collection.

The French Tapestry Colour
Les couleurs de la tapisserie français

Depuis 1770
Yardley

bien colours are drawn from

For a fresh, natural look
French Tapestry combination.
Start with Creamy Beige foundation.
colour to your cheeks with Hickory Indian
For eyeshadow, apply matte-brush Indian Tobacco
blended with a Flowering Currant Brown. To
highlight brown, add matte Vanilla. For lips, Frosted
Bamboo Rose. Then add the finishing touch with
frosted Wood Sorrel nail polish.

Pour avoir ce teint éclatant de fraîcheur cet
automne, adoptez cette «tapisserie française».
Commencez par appliquer un fond de teint
Creamy Beige et rehaussez vos pommettes de fard
d'un fard en poudre Hickory. Ombrez vos paupières
soupçon de Flowering Currant Brown mélangé d'un
léger en valeur appliquant un Vanille. Pour les lèvres vos
avec une touche de Bamboo Rose très Frosté
frottant en velours de brillant Arrowhead Brown.
frottant ou en application du vernis à ongles nacré
Wood Sorrel.

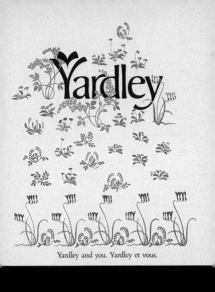

Yardley and you. Yardley et vous.

2 Perfumed bath soaps
Savons de bain parfumés

Since Depuis 1770
Yardley
Roses

2x150g

Roses
3x50g

Roses
3x100g

Since Depuis 1770
Yardley
Roses

500g
Moisturizing
bath salts
Sels de bain
hydratants

Since Depuis 1770
Yardley
Roses

150g
Perfumed
Talc
parfumé

hand soaps
mains parfumés

3 Perfumed hand soaps
Savons à mains parfumés

Since Depuis 1770
Yardley
Lotus

3x100g

Lotus
2x150g

Since Depuis 1770
Yardley
Lotus

Since Depuis 1770
Yardley
Lotus

500g
Moisturizing
bath salts
Sels de bain
hydratants

150g
Perfumed
Talc
parfumé

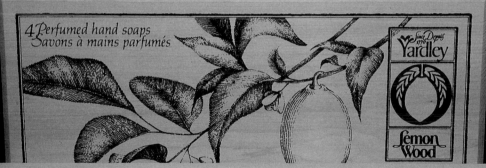

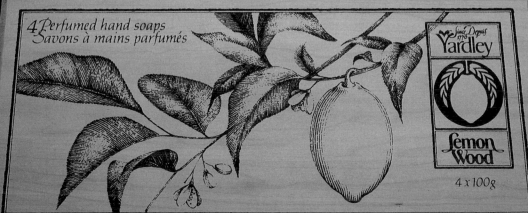

3 Perfumed hand soaps
Savons à mains parfumés

Since Depuis 1770
Yardley

Lemon Wood

3 x 100g

5 Perfumed guest soaps
Savons parfumés pour invités

Since Depuis 1770
Yardley

Lemon Wood

5 x 50 g

3 Perfumed hand soaps
Savons à mains parfumés

Since Depuis 1770
Yardley

SeaMist

3 x 100g

5 Perfumed guest soaps
Savons parfumés pour invités

Since Depuis 1770
Yardley

SeaMist

5 x 50 g

Kimberly-Clark learned long ago that listening to customers can be very good for business. To meet the shortage of surgical cotton during World War I, the company invented a crepe cellulose substitute. Almost immediately, U.S. Army nurses began using the new product as disposable sanitary napkins – the world's first. Kimberly-Clark took note and, when the war ended, brought out a new product called Kotex in a plain brown wrapper.

The company's other major product, Kleenex, also did well when the market discovered new uses for it. Kleenex tissues were put on the market in 1924 as "cold cream removers" and sold at the incredibly high price of 65 cents a pack. Before long, customers discovered that these "towels" could also be used as disposable handkerchiefs. But the high price was a deterrent.

Kimberly-Clark responded with a lower price, a new pop-up box, and – as far back as 1929 – tissues in pink, green, and yellow, as well as in white.

By the time that I became involved with the Kleenex line, more than 50 years later, the "decorator pack" had been well established and Kimberly-Clark had found that revising the design every few years kept it current with prevailing tastes.

This is an interesting medium for an artist because, unlike most other packaging, its sole objective is to appear as pleasing to the eye as possible. (The typography simply fits into an existing oval that the customer pops out and throws away.)

But because the design of the package has such an impact on sales, great care has to be taken to ensure that the look is just right. I made colored mock-ups in the shape of the box so that no one would have to guess as to how the illustration would be applied.

Above: Butterflies, one of the proposed designs that didn't fly.

In keeping with its longstanding tradition of listening to the people who keep them in business, Kimberly-Clark submits its designs to a research company, which gets opinions from 200 or 300 members of the public.

That can be a nerve-wracking experience for an artist; it's like standing in front of 200 or 300 jurors. But of the dozen or so designs that I submitted, I felt that two stood out above the rest. When the verdict came down, I was pleased to learn that these were the same two that the jury liked best.

Facing Page: (Above) Wildflowers. Oil painting on board. This kind of imagery, which represents some of my favorite wild flowers, demands considerable skill from the printers. With the high speeds at which today's presses run, it would be very easy for the image to fall out of register, which would blur the design and ruin the look of the product in the store.

(Below) Geometric Lace. The inspiration for this package came from a piece of lace that I had stretched over a stairwell window in my home to hide the brick wall behind it. I drew the lace by following a very tight grid, which made the pattern bolder and more graphic. As the background is just two colors, this is a much easier package to print than the one above.

White **Kleenex** *Blanc*
100 2 Ply Tissues • 100 Mouchoirs 2 épaisseurs • 21 x 21 cm

Kleenex *Blanc*
100 Mouchoirs 2 épaisseurs • 21 x 21 cm

White **Kleenex** *Blanc*
100 2 Ply Tissues • 100 Mouchoirs 2 épaisseurs • 21 x 21 cm

Kleenex *Blanc*
• 100 Mouchoirs 2 épaisseurs • 21 x 21 cm

Many people assume that Crabtree & Evelyn is a European business. In fact, it's based in Connecticut and managed by an astute team of American marketers.

In 1981, Crabtree & Evelyn had just purchased a small manufacturer of quality jams and jellies, Scarborough & Company, and wanted to launch a new line of products with labels based on early American folk art.

I was asked to create paintings for the jams and stencil-designs for the jellies.

The first thing that I had to do was to learn about American folk art. I bought every book that I could get my hands on, and pored over as many primitive paintings as I could find, learning how various techniques were executed. This gave me the knowledge and confidence that I needed.

The paintings were enthusiastically received by the client, but the stencil-designs didn't work nearly as well. They fell flat by comparison with the paintings. It may have been the limitations of the subject matter or the space with which I had to work; I still can't say for sure. All I know is that they were not sufficiently cap-tivating to launch a product line.

As a result, the stencil-design idea was abandoned and we continued with the paintings.

When the product line was completed, we learned another important lesson. To finish off the package we had decided to add a small paper cap to cover the lid. On the cap appeared a painted logo of a basket of fruit against an elegant black background. It looked wonderful on paper, but all too often the black would get scuffed or scraped in shipping, and by the time it was unpacked it just didn't create the impression of quality we had hoped for. The solution was a printed metal lid that kept the same image. It doesn't have the cachet of the paper cap, but it gets to the stores in better shape.

Above: Fruit basket identifier for Scarborough & Company's jam jars. This image was reproduced in color on metal lids and a decorative paper wrap (since abandoned).

Below: Detail from the Black Cherry *painting, oil on board. Private collection.*

Facing Page: The complete line of jams.

Page 86: Fruit basket painted in the style of early American art, oil on board. Private collection.

Pages 87 and 88: Paintings for Scarborough & Company labels: apricot, blueberry, strawberry, peach, blackberry, and rose hip, oil on board. Private collection.

R BOROUG
PRICOT JAM

net wt 340 g 12 OZ poids net 255 ml 9 oz fl

SCARBOROUGH
BLACK BING CHERRY JAM

net wt 340 g 12 OZ poids net 255 ml 9 oz fl

SCARBO
BLUEBERRY JA

net wt 340 g 12 OZ poids net 255 ml 9 o

ARBOROUG
ASPBERRY CURRANT JELLY
net wt 340 g 12 OZ poids net 255 ml 9 fl

AP AT FOUR POINTS AROUND LID TO OPEN
ARBOROUGH
STRAWBERRY JELLY
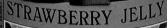

net wt 340 g 12 OZ poids net 255 ml 9 oz fl

AT FOUR POINTS AROUND LID TO OPEN
ARBOROUGH
RED RASPBERRY JA

net wt 340 g 12 OZ poids net 255 ml 9 o

R BOROUGH SARBOROUGH
TRAWBERRY JAM
net wt 340 g 12 OZ poids net 255 ml 9 fl

AP AT FOUR POINTS AROUND LID TO OPEN
ARBOROUGH
ELDERBERRY JELLY
net wt 340 g 12 OZ poids net 255 ml 9 oz fl

AT FOUR POINTS AROUND LID TO OPEN
ARBOROUGH
BLACKBERRY JA
net wt 340 g 12 OZ poids net 255 ml 9

SARBOROUGH
ROSE HIP JELLY

net wt 340 g 12 OZ poids net 255 ml 9 fl

AT FOUR POINTS AROUND LID TO OPEN
SCARBOROUGH
PEACH JAM

net wt 340 g 12 OZ poids net 255 ml 9 oz fl

ARBOROUGH
BLACK RASPBERRY JELL
net wt 340 g 12 OZ poids net 255 ml 9

It must be the dream of most people to go into business for themselves. And of those who do, it sometimes seems as if a significant percentage get in touch with me. This may be because packaging is usually one of the first requirements for any new enterprise, and would-be entrepreneurs will often approach a design studio before they visit an advertising agency – sometimes even before they know the first thing about advertising and promotion.

It's easy to waste a lot of time handholding beginners whose businesses never quite get off the ground.

Today, I'm a little embarrassed to admit that I once put Eleanor Sigona in that category. Eleanor, who lives in McLean, Virginia, had seen some of my work and thought that I'd be able to help her launch The Perfect Taste, a new line of herbal seasonings that she planned to turn out. Apart from the fact that she grew her own basil, Eleanor seemed ill-suited to succeed at such an ambitious undertaking. She knew little about the intricacies of packaging and merchandising, and I found it hard to take her seriously.

That was a mistake. To begin with, Eleanor had a wonderful product. Her seasonings were not only salt-free, they had none of the sodium substitutes that are often used to supply the taste of salt. Instead, she had skillfully blended a variety of tastes that suggested the presence of salt with none of its harmful effects.

As well as having a good product, Eleanor believed in what she was doing, and was convinced that she could get her product distributed in specialty shops and in the gourmet sections of food chains. I have tremendous respect for that kind of against-all-odds determination.

When we agreed to get together, we met in New York City. She preferred

Above: Herbal bouquet for lids and labels.

Below: Perfect Taste wordmark.

Page 90: The full product line.

Page 91: Perfect Taste labels; note the list of ingredients.

it to Toronto, and I preferred it to McLean, Virginia.

Believing, quite correctly, that tasting the product would be a useful step in preparing to do the artwork, Eleanor brought some samples to my suite at The Regency. Unfortunately, she brought them in small plastic bags, the kind frequently used by traffickers of certain controlled substances. I remember thinking that if anyone at Canada Customs were to check my luggage I'd be sure to end up on the wrong side of a drug bust. I also remember thinking, "No, that's ridiculous; these are legitimate product samples and I need them for my work." In the end, I confess, my eagerness to avoid a scene at the airport won out. The samples were unceremoniously dumped in a Regency wastebasket.

the Perfect Taste
HERBAL
SEASONINGS
NO SALT
GARDEN
BOUQUET
A Rich Blend of Natural Herbs
net wt 2.25 oz 64g

the Perfect Taste
HERBAL
SEASONINGS
NO SALT
PIQUANT
A Hot, Spicy Herbal Mixture
net wt 1.6 oz 45g

the Perfect Taste
HERBAL
SEASONINGS
NO SALT
SAVOURY BLEND
The Natural Salt Substitute
net wt 2.25 oz 64g

HERBAL SEASONINGS FROM
THE PERFECT TASTE

the Perfect Taste

HERBAL SEASONINGS

NO. SALT

SAVOURY BLEND

The Natural Salt Substitute

net wt 2.25 oz 64 g

A specially created blend of natural herbs and spices used as an all purpose seasoning in cooking or at the table as an alternative to salt. Sprinkle generously to add an enticing livelier flavor.

Ingredients: Powdered lemon juice, onion powder, oregano, basil, anise.

For recipes write to:
The Perfect Taste
6722 Curran Street
McLean, Virginia 22101

---

the Perfect Taste

HERBAL SEASONINGS

NO. SALT

PIQUANT

A Hot, Spicy Herbal Mixture

net wt 1.6 oz 45 g

Sprinkle generously on meats, fish, poultry, and vegetables, paté, eggs, and sauces. Stir fry, marinate, barbecue. Let your imagination go.

Ingredients: Parsley, white pepper, sesame seed, paprika, garlic powder, onion, rosemary, oregano, thyme, red pepper, cumin, mustard powder, cinnamon, allspice.

For recipes write to:
The Perfect Taste
6722 Curran Street
McLean, Virginia 22101

If Ernest D'Israeli Smith hadn't suffered from poor eyesight at an early age, he might have continued his studies to become an engineer. Instead he became a farmer. And if his wife hadn't objected on religious grounds, he might have then gone into winemaking. Instead, he started a cannery and watched it grow into one of Canada's largest and most respected food companies.

When I became involved with E. D. Smith and Sons, Limited the company had just celebrated its 100th anniversary, yet the Smith family still held a strong presence. My contact was Llewellyn S. Smith, who would soon become the president.

Our relationship began with the development of a new graphic identity. This, I soon realized, was more than just another corporate name. This was a family name, and the wordmark had to represent not just a line of products but the family itself, and all that the family stood for.

The solution came in three parts: First was the wordmark with its strongly Canadian theme. Next came a hallmark of quality, which reflected the company's farming community roots. The third component was the guarantee that announced, loudly and clearly, that behind this company were people who cared about the products that carried its name.

Once the identity was established, we turned our attention to package design. Food processing is a very seasonal industry; once the season passes for any one product, the next opportunity for photography is months away.

And there is little point in working on photography before the package design has been approved. Not only must the fruit be shown so that it looks its best in terms of light and shadow, it must also be free from conflicting highlights in those areas where the photo becomes a back-

Above: Corporate identifier for E. D. Smith & Sons.

Center: The hallmark of quality.

Below: English and French logos for Lite 'n Fruity, *a low-sugar pie filling. It's rare for a wordmark to be this compatible in both official languages.*

Facing Page: Philip Rostron's photograph for the apple pie filling label.

Page 94: (Above) Packaging for E. D. Smith pie filling.

(Below) Packaging for Lite 'n Fruity.

Page 95: Photograph for raspberry pie filling.

Page 96: Packaging for E. D. Smith jams and jellies.

Page 97: (Above) Packaging for E. D. Smith marmalades.

(Below) Strawberry and blueberry labels for E. D. Smith jams.

Page 98 and 99: Photograph for strawberry and peach pie filling.

ground for type, particularly smaller type. This is more of a challenge in Canada than in most other countries because two official languages invariably dictate a good deal of type on our packaging. Until the design is completed, no one knows where those background areas will fall.

But if the photography is left too late in the season, it can lead to the kind of problems that we encountered. We had photographed Montmorency cherries for the pie filling but didn't realize that we'd need another shot for the cherry jam. An exhaustive search through the orchards for more cherries turned up precisely two, the last two cherries of the season. Fortunately, computer technology helped us to repeat the photo of those two cherries in a way that looked quite natural and appealing. A very close call.

In food photography, the relationship between designer and photographer is everything. On this assignment, I worked with Philip Rostron of Toronto. Between us we learned what a cantankerous subject the humble blueberry can be when it's asked to pose for a photograph. Blueberries have a surface much like a fine nap. Pick one up and fingerprints remain. Bounce them among other berries and you'll leave visible blotches. At one point I tried to cover the blotches by dusting them with a paintbrush and talcum powder. The result was blueberries that looked as if someone had dusted them with a paintbrush and talcum powder.

No wonder food photography is so expensive. Few subjects are less forgiving in the wrong hands. Only when you see how good food can look when it's been captured by an expert do you realize that it really is worth the time and trouble.

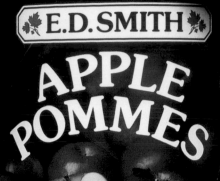

E.D. SMITH
LEMON
250 mL
SPREAD

E.D. SMITH
THREE FRUIT
250 mL
PURE MARMALADE

E.D. SMITH
ORANGE
250 mL
SPREAD

E.D. SMITH
FRAISES
250 mL
CONFITURE PURE

Ingredients
Strawberries blended
with corn syrup, sugar,
citric acid & pectin.

Ingrédients
Fraises mélangées avec
sirop de maïs, sucre,
acide citrique et pectine.

No preservatives added.
Sans preservatifs.

E.D. SMITH
STRAWBERRY
250 mL
PURE JAM

E.D. SMITH & SONS, LTD.
E.D. SMITH & FILS, LTÉE.
WINONA, ONTARIO
CANADA L0R 2L0

0   670682   COR 65

E.D. SMITH
BLEUETS
250 mL
CONFITURE PURE

Ingredients
Blueberries blended
with corn syrup, sugar,
pectin & citric acid.

Ingrédients
Bleuets mélangés avec
sirop de maïs, sucre,
pectine et acide citrique.

No preservatives added.
Sans preservatifs.

E.D. SMITH
BLUEBERRY
250 mL
PURE JAM

E.D. SMITH & SONS, LTD.
E.D. SMITH & FILS, LTÉE.
WINONA, ONTARIO
CANADA L0R 2L0

0   670612   COR 65

One of the most extraordinary success stories in recent business history belongs to Roots. The company began in 1971, when Don Green and Michael Budman, two Detroit expatriates in their twenties, tried to bring the Earth Shoe into Canada. Some will remember Earth Shoes for their negative heels, wide toes, and sundry bodily blessings. In a move they would later regret, Earth Shoe executives in the United States turned the young men down.

For many people that would have been the end of it. But Don and Michael decided to have their own shoes made in Canada, where they were now living and where their emotional ties went back to boyhood summers in Ontario's Algonquin Provincial Park.

They started looking in the Yellow Pages for manufacturers, and got as far as the 'B's, where they found Boa Shoe, a small family-run factory in Toronto's West End.

It proved a wonderful relationship. The shoe took off and within months there were more than a hundred Roots shops across North America and Europe. Stores selling the rival Earth Shoe soon disappeared from sight.

As negative heels ran their course, Roots evolved into other footwear and fashions, always emphasizing a natural look, with colours from the Canadian north: greens, tans, and earth and mineral shades.

My role began before the first store opened. The partners had come up with the name Roots on their own and needed a graphic identity. We agreed at the start that whatever we did a beaver would be part of the design. This was an ideal choice as the beaver symbolizes Canada, particularly the north, and is well known for its industrious habits.

Clearly, a static logo would have been most inappropriate for this

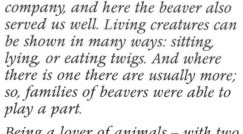
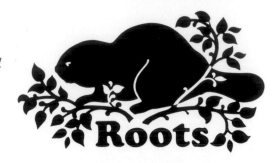

Above: Roots graphic identity. This silhouette was one of five that were used everywhere from shoe soles to signage. The degree of complexity in the art depended upon the final application.

Below: Pen and ink drawings depicting the beaver in a natural setting. Two from a series of six illustrations used to reinforce Roots graphic identity.

Facing page: The Roots Beaver, 1976, oil on canvas, 18¼ by 18 in. The image appeared on two editions of posters, 1976 and 1986. Roots of Canada collection.

Page 102: Roots saddle-soap lid.

Page 103: Roots packaging, demonstrating the versatility of the beaver as a symbol.

Page 104: The Loon. From Roots Northern Lakes and Woodlands *clothing line.*

Page 105: Three of the seven designs in the Northern Lakes and Woodlands *series.*

company, and here the beaver also served us well. Living creatures can be shown in many ways: sitting, lying, or eating twigs. And where there is one there are usually more; so, families of beavers were able to play a part.

Being a lover of animals – with two dogs and four cats at home – I found this a particularly satisfying assignment. It helped that Roots products were sold in their own shops: this way packages could be designed to look their best, without our having to worry about the need to "out scream" competitive brands.

Placing an emphasis on strong graphics right from the beginning would help Roots to benefit from a remarkable phenomenon in later years. Had anyone told me, when I was going to school, that a future status symbol in teen fashion would be a sweat shirt promoting a clothing business, I would have thought they were crazy. Yet that's exactly what happened with Roots, and as I write this it's still happening, as young boys and girls volunteer themselves as mini mobile billboards.

For all my years in the business, I'm at a loss to explain it. But I do take comfort in knowing that other businesses, applying less thoughtful graphics, have tried the same thing and failed.

ROOTS
NORTHERN·LAKES

Imperial Oil, for a long time the largest petroleum company in Canada, is 70 percent owned by Exxon. But Imperial has always been able to look even the most ardent Canadian nationalists in the eye. One reason: the company has been in business here since 1880 and rarely misses an opportunity to remind Canadians of the role it has played in the country's development. It usually achieves this with a great deal of taste. For example, the major project for Imperial's 100th birthday in 1980 was a series of seven television specials on Canada's founding peoples. It cost the company $7 million to produce and air the series; yet, the only commercial announcement ran at the beginning of the first program – to explain why there would be no more commercial interruptions!

For Imperial's annual report that year, I was asked to develop a brief history of the company's exploration, refining, and marketing activities.

I began with all the obvious sources: company and government archives, and history books. But there wasn't enough material to get a clear picture of the industry's early days. For that I had to travel to western Ontario, where Canada's oil boom began.

Although Edwin Drake is usually credited with drilling North America's first commercial oil well near Titusville, Pennsylvania in 1859, his was not the first successful well. That record belongs to James Miller Williams who sunk his well two years earlier at what is now Oil Springs, Ontario. And Williams did his the hard way, not by drilling but by digging.

Today, the area around Oil Springs and neighboring communities such as Petrolia depend more on farming than on petroleum. But there are still hundreds of working pumps to be

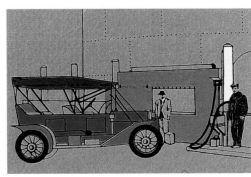

Working from the visual reference material that I acquired, I prepared a series of pencil drawings, adding people to give the drawings life. Once these were approved, they were completed as pen and ink renderings; some areas were painted to enhance the overall image.

found – some of them in fields of corn – and the memories of many older people still brim with recollections of the oil business as it once was.

I flew into nearby Sarnia, and for the better part of a week wandered the area in a rented car. I talked to pensioners who had worked the oil fields themselves. I met people whose family albums had pictures of relatives who had worked there. One old gentleman took me to visit a friend whose barn housed an ancient steam engine that once ran the old wooden drilling rigs. I even came away with a photograph of "Old Man Time", the nickname for the worker who trimmed the grass between the rigs with a scythe. The whole experience was like a visit to another age.

Inevitably, my search for relics from the days of the oil boom led me into numerous junk shops and antique stores, where all resistance failed me. I ended up with many items that I needed as visual reference for the project, and many more that I didn't, including two carpets, a big silver spoon, four salt-glazed pitchers, and an old-time powder keg. The only way that I could get everything back was by cashing in the return half of my plane ticket and taking the rented car home.

Middle Column: (Above) This detail from The History of Marketing *depicts a tank wagon waiting to load up at an early refinery before setting out on its rounds to customers. With the arrival of the internal combustion engine, drivers of the first automobiles were soon squeezing into line among the delivery wagons. These new customers proved such a nuisance at the Imperial Oil depot in Vancouver that in 1907 the manager attached a garden hose to a water tank, and filled the tank with gasoline so that horseless carriages could be serviced outside. Thus was born the world's first gasoline station.*

(Below) Historic graphic identifier for Imperial Oil.

Facing Page: The History of Exploration.

Page 108: The History of Refining.

One of the words that people in our business hate to hear from a client is "collage". Some advertisers can't make up their mind as to which of several items should be shown, and believe that a collection of unrelated images will cover all bases. At other times, company politics may necessitate products from a number of different departments being represented in an image. Companies sometimes forget that the average North American consumer is exposed to more than 1,800 advertising messages a day, which makes it madness to go with anything less than the strongest possible visual presentation.

Collages can be difficult enough to get right even when there's a legitimate reason for using them – even in a medium where your page does not have to fight for attention. We proved this in the 1981 annual report for Imperial Oil.

Imperial, like a growing number of companies, has recognized the full potential of the annual report as a communications vehicle. Done right, it can be a useful and persuasive medium, not just for shareholders and the investment community, but also for government regulators, the press, employees, and potential recruits.

In 1981, Imperial Oil wanted to make a number of important points and needed a photograph for each. The areas of interest included natural resources, petroleum products, chemicals, human resources, and the company as a good corporate citizen. The client would supply all the items to be photographed for each page.

I assigned Philip Rostron to handle the photography because I knew that he was used to handling tall orders. But when the products started coming in from Imperial, it became very clear that we were going to have our work cut out for us.

Above: For the section on fuels, we needed hose nozzles, but all we could get were used ones. Each had to be taken apart, sandblasted, polished, and reassembled. Then we painted them in brilliant colors to get the effect we wanted.

Pages 110 and 111: The annual report cover: a little bit of everything brought together.

Page 112: Photograph for Natural Resources.

The photograph covering natural resources, for example, included crude oil from tar sands, conventional crude oil, natural gas, copper ore and copper ore concentrate, coal, and sulfur. We decided to use powdered sulfur and discovered that it's just like working with very fine flour, except that it's yellow. The slightest movement in the studio sends clouds of the stuff into the air and all over the other components of the shot.

We decided to try a large sulfur rock instead, and paid $250 to have one shipped down from Northern Ontario. Unfortunately, it was ugly, enormous, and contained very little sulfur. We went back to the powder and finally persuaded it to behave.

For another shot, we had to include a segment of muskeg. Muskeg is the peat-like substance that covers millions of square miles of the Canadian north. Our sample was still cold when it arrived at the studio. But under the hot lights it suddenly sprang to life and hundreds of creeping, slithering creatures–bugs you'll never find in a Raid commercial–emerged from the muskeg and scurried all over the set.

For the cover of the annual report, the challenge was a little more severe: we had to do a composite that included something from each of the other collections.

But looking back on the effort years later, I must admit that I'm pleased with the results. Maybe all those clients who keep pushing for collages know what they're doing after all!

People who aren't in the advertising or graphic arts business can have a hard time figuring out exactly what someone like me does for a living. I suspect that part of the confusion lies in the fact that I not only design ads, posters, and brochures, but often produce the illustrations and paintings that appear in them. That's not very common.

But my knowledge of other media, such as the technical side of photography, for example, is quite limited. Yet as long as I can communicate with photographers I can get the effect that I'm after.

The puzzle box shown here is a perfect example of creating an idea for an unfamiliar medium, then having it properly executed by a professional. I designed it as a gift for a special friend who was fond of puzzles. I knew what I wanted and I knew the puzzles that the box should contain. To bring it to life, I called in Paul Epp, a Canadian artist and craftsman who works in wood.

First came the box, which fits together like a puzzle itself. When that was nearly completed, we worked on the puzzles so, that each drawer could be designed accordingly. Some spaces were left so that more puzzles could be added in the future.

Because each component needed its own set of instructions, I assigned one to each member of my staff. No two designers will tackle a problem in exactly the same way, thank goodness; so, I ended up with a pleasing variety of different approaches. It added one more dimension to the uniqueness of the gift.

Today, there are people who spend bundles of money in trendy boutiques in search of "the perfect gift". If only they knew how much more satisfaction there is in starting with an original idea and seeing an artist turn it into reality.

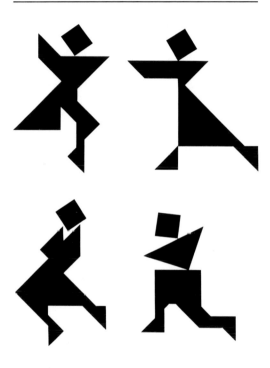

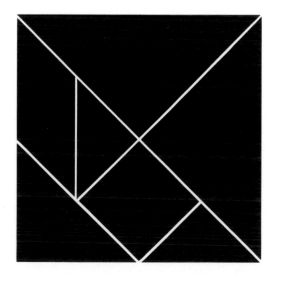

Middle Column: (Above) The puzzle box nearly closed.

(Below) Tangram, a Chinese puzzle game; each dancing figure must use all seven pieces, touching without overlapping.

Page 114: The puzzle box opening; note the interior drawers.

Page 115: The puzzle box fully opened, with its puzzles and handmade instructions.

TANGRAM
A CHINESE PUZZLE GAME
FOR ROBERT BURNS

The world's first postage stamp was designed by Britain's Sir Rowland Hill, who in 1840 invented the idea of postage stamps along with the Universal Postal System. The world's first pictorial stamp was Canada's three-penny beaver, designed in 1851 by Sir Sandford Fleming, the much-celebrated railway surveyor who also came up with the idea of standard time. Distinguished company indeed. Small wonder that I welcomed an invitation to design stamps for Canada Post Corporation. I have been fascinated by stamps for some time and my collection includes one of Sir Sandford's three-penny beavers (unfortunately not the one that's worth a lot of money).

From the point of view of pure unadulterated ego, it numbs the mind to picture a billion stamps flying to all corners of the world carrying my illustrations. I'm also touched by the idea of work that enjoys an afterlife in the collections of future generations.

My series on wildflowers and trees became Canada's "definitive", or official daily stamps from 1977 to 1982. The first step was the creation of a precise line drawing of each plant for the approval of a team of government-appointed botanists. Then the color areas were delineated, and the line details that give each image its form and texture were prepared as separate pen and ink drawings. The line artwork was then printed on top of the flat color by a steel engraved plate to produce the finished stamp.

The double printing process is intended to discourage forgers. So is the rule that prevents me from repro-ducing my stamps here without the little thin line across them. The other choice would have been to print them 50 percent larger than life – but that would have meant blowing up some-thing that had already been printed, which would make the images fuzzy.

Although the double printing process makes forgery more difficult it also creates problems in reproduction. When the engraving plate overprints the colored areas it connects with considerable pressure; sometimes the paper gives beneath its weight and moves a little. As a result, if you examine these stamps under a magnifying glass, as collectors often do, you'll notice that the engraved drawing doesn't always match with the colored areas.

Nevertheless, the system offers designers much more flexibility than the straight engraving process that was used until 1967; before then, Canadian stamps were limited to just one or two colors and a series like this wouldn't have worked nearly as well.

Middle Column: (Above) Definitive wild flower stamps: 1¢ Bottle Gentian; 2¢ Western Columbine; 3¢ Canadian Lily; 4¢ Hepatica; 5¢ Shooting Star; 10¢ Sparrow's Egg Lady's Slipper; 12¢ Jewel Weed; 15¢ Canadian Violet.

(Center) Definitive tree stamps: 15¢ Trembling Aspen; 25¢ Sugar Maple; 30¢ Red Oak; 35¢ Eastern White Pine.

(Below) Commemorative horticultural stamp.

Facing page: The Garden, oil on board, 1980. Archives of Canada Post Corporation. With commemorative stamps, forgery is less of a concern because of their shorter life span. Usually, a painting is commissioned and the artwork must be about five times as large as the stamp. Image reproduction, courtesy of Canada Post Corporation.

Posters are to the artist what film is to the actor or books to the writer. Posters let you share your work with thousands of people who might otherwise not have the chance to enjoy it.

Without posters, an artist's audience would be limited to the select few who can afford private collections of original art, or to the relatively small numbers who frequent galleries.

Art deserves a wider audience than that. And people other than those who can afford to buy paintings deserve the pleasures of art in the home.

Posters, by virtue of their accessibility and relatively low cost, have become the art form of choice for many North Americans. Sometimes, as in the celebration of a theater performance, the poster is a reminder of a joyful event. But most often it is selected simply because it pleases the eye. Whatever the reason, posters are important to those artists who like the idea of their work reaching out to wider numbers.

I have always been one of those artists, believing that the people who most appreciate my work are not the elitist few, but people of all income levels in every walk of life.

Middle Column: (Above) The Crane, *1979, oil on board.*

(Below) The Insects, *1979, oil on board.*

Facing Page: Couples, *1977, oil on canvas, 24 by 24 in. Promotional poster for the Jamaican resort. Some who are less than intimate with the mating habits of lions took this to be a representation of intercourse. But the animals are simply cuddling (as the casual positioning of the lioness's tail should confirm). This is the original version of the poster. Printing had already been completed when the client ordered the breasts on the female to be painted out, and all existing copies of the first press run destroyed. But judging from the number that I keep running into, dozens of the original version seem to have broken free before the mastectomy. Private collection.*

Page 120: The Silver Apples, *oil on canvas, 18 by 24 in. Commissioned in 1982 by Leo Burnett Advertising, Toronto. The client*

wanted a limited edition of posters incorporating the agency's symbol, the apple. I based this image on a William Butler Yeats poem that reads:
    And pluck till time and times are done
    The silver apples of the moon,
    the golden apples of the sun.
I felt that the verse fairly represented what the agency and its clients were in business to do. Private collection.

Page 121: Orchids, *1979, oil on board.*

Pages 122 and 123: The White Tigers, *oil on canvas, 28 by 28 in. Commissioned in 1983 to celebrate the purchase of two young white tigers by the Houston Zoological Society. Posters were distributed at a fund-raising dinner. The original painting was auctioned*

to raise money for the upkeep of the tigers. The Blanton Collection, Houston.

Pages 124 and 125: Guelph, *oil on canvas, 48 by 48 in. Commissioned in 1981 by the University of Guelph, Canada's leading center of agricultural learning. The Hanoverian horse stands for the agricultural side of learning, and the black Pegasus represents the arts side of the curriculum. The Franklin Collection*

Page 126: Connections, *oil on canvas, 19 by 24 in. Commissioned in 1982 by Simpson Paper Company, San Francisco. Private collection.*

Page 127: Scollard, *oil on canvas, 24 1/2 by 35 1/2 in. Commissioned in 1985 by Scollard Films, Toronto. Private collection.*

Page 128: The Doll, *oil on canvas, 25 by 37 in. Private collection.*

Page 129: Great Expectations, *oil on canvas, 28 by 46 in. Commissioned in 1987 by North York (Ontario) Mayor Mel Lastman and his wife Marilyn, in honor of the Ontario Games for the Physically Disabled. Olympia and York Collection.*

Page 130: Pan, *oil on board, 11 1/2 by 13 1/2 in. Private collection.*

Page 131: The Montgolfier Balloon, *oil on canvas, 22 1/2 by 17 1/2 in. Commissioned in 1986 by The Partnership, Atlanta, on behalf of the Associated Aviation Underwriters, New York. The collection of the Associated Aviation Underwriters.*

Pages 132 and 133: Allergy, *oil on canvas, 17 1/2 by 39 in. Commissioned in 1986 by Vicom/FCB on behalf of Syntex Laboratories Inc. The collection of Syntex Laboratories Inc.*

Page 134: Expo '86, *oil and acrylic on canvas, 24 by 34 1/2 in. Commissioned in 1985 by the 1986 World Exposition, Vancouver. The collection of the 1986 World Exposition.*

Page 135: The Basilisk, *pen and ink on paper, 24 by 36 1/2 in., 1985. This image was created for a limited edition of silk-screen posters. It was contributed to the Shoshin Society for the Hiroshima Memorial Services which, takes place each year in Japan. The silk-screen printers, Holland and Neil Limited, also contributed their time and expertise to this project. Private collection.*

COUPLES

NOW. THE COUPLE TAKES ITS RIGHTFUL PLACE IN THE SUN.

EXPO 86

The 1986
World Exposition
Vancouver
British Columbia, Canada
May 2 - October 13, 1986

Exposition internationale
de 1986
Vancouver
Colombie-Britannique, Canada
Du 2 mai au 13 octobre 1986

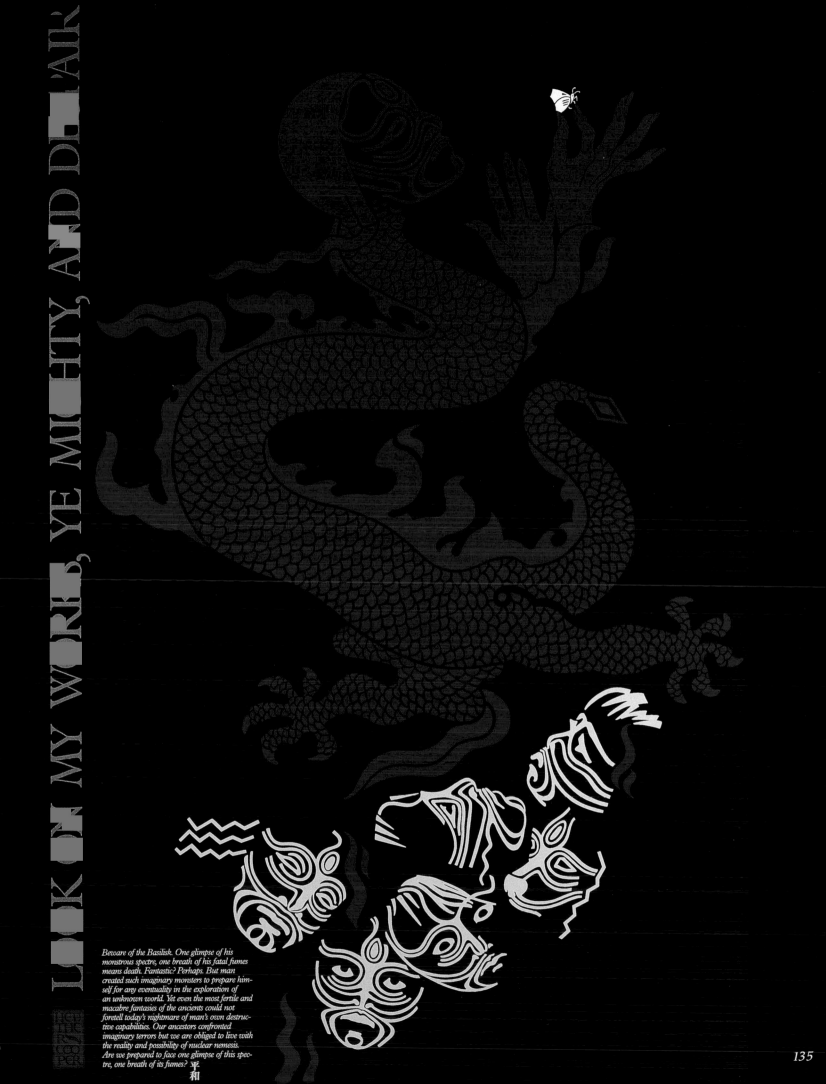

LOOK ON MY WORLD, YE MIGHTY, AND DESPAIR

Beware of the Basilisk. One glimpse of his
monstrous spectre, one breath of his fatal fumes
means death. Fantastic? Perhaps. But man
created such imaginary monsters to prepare himself for any eventuality in the exploration of
an unknown world. Yet even the most fertile and
macabre fantasies of the ancients could not
foretell today's nightmare of man's own destruc-
tive capabilities. Our ancestors confronted
imaginary terrors but we are obliged to live with
the reality and possibility of nuclear nemesis.
Are we prepared to face one glimpse of this spectre, one breath of its fumes?

Direct mail may be the least respected of today's advertising media. The problem lies largely in the company that it keeps. At our house, a typical stack of mail usually begins with a nightmarish flier for aluminum siding and ends with an envelope stuffed with homely typefaces announcing: "You, Ms. Heather Cooper, may have won…" four or five times per page.

Unwillingness to be linked to that kind of image may be keeping a lot of responsible companies out of direct mail. And that's a shame because for some marketing programs it really can't be beaten.

Provincial Papers is a wonderful example of a company that does it well. For almost 20 years, I've been associated with the group that markets their fine papers and I've learned a good deal from them about intelligent salesmanship.

Their audience, by and large, is people like me whose job includes the specification of paper. Direct mail not only keeps Provincial Papers' name in front of its customers, it also circulates samples of the company's products. And by using a highly graphic approach – usually in the form of posters – the company ensures that its mailings are seen by more than the person whose name is on the envelope.

These would be reasons enough to justify the use of direct mail; but Provincial Papers goes even further by explaining to readers all of the technical details on how the material was put together. The advantage of this is two-fold. First, it makes readers more knowledgeable and therefore a little more comfortable with the product. But, second, it also communicates in no uncertain terms that this is a company that knows its way around the graphic arts business and speaks the reader's language.

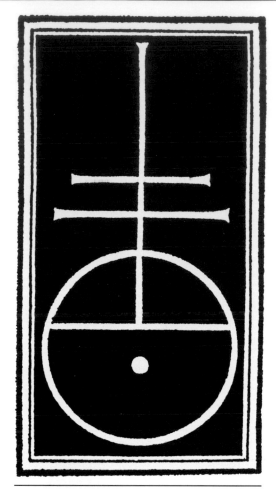

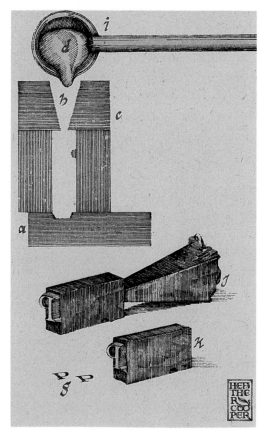

Middle Column: (Above) Graphic identifier used by Nicholas Jenson, the French engraver who revived and redesigned the characters of the Roman alphabet, which have remained essentially unchanged to this day. This is a detail from The Coated Classics, a series of posters that made up a 1976 direct mail program.

(Below) and facing page: Details from the pen and ink drawing, "How to Cast Type". From The Coated Classics, 1976.

Page 138: Winged Fish, oil on canvas, 25 by 37 in. Private collection. This image appeared in a brochure that opened into a poster. It depicted the similarity between the forms in nature and a sailboat. For me it does much more, symbolizing the ability to fly through the air as well as to dive to the depths of the ocean; but an effort to accomplish both at once leaves the creature helplessly suspended between the two.

Page 139: The Rime of the Ancient Mariner, one of a series of preliminary pencil sketches based on the poem by Samuel Taylor Coleridge. When I was at this stage of the work the product that we were promoting was discontinued and the project was abandoned.

Thou hast most traitorously corrupted the youth of the realm in erecting a grammar school: and whereas, before, our forefathers had no other books but the score and the tally, thou hast caused printing to be used, and, contrary to the king, his crown and dignity, thou hast built a paper mill.
Shakespeare; King Henry VI, Part II

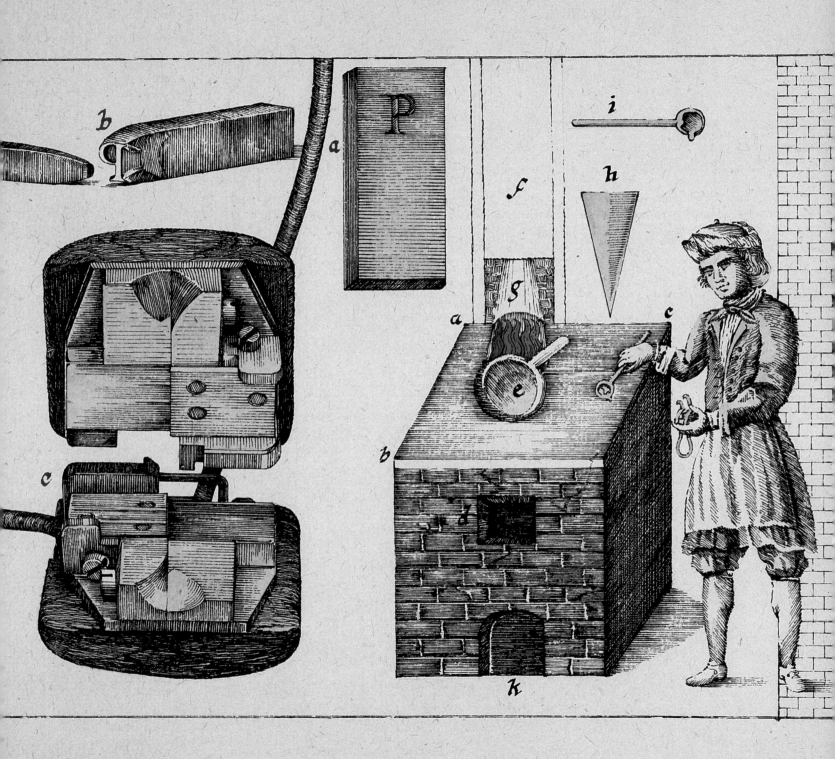

"What is there in thee, Moon! that thou should'st move My heart so potently? John Keats

Long before the arrival of street lamps and sealed-beam headlights, the moon was man's most important ally in finding his way around after dark. Understandably, primitive people regarded the moon with reverence, and saw its changing faces as religious omens. Juno, the Roman moon goddess, was by derivation appointed goddess of childbirth and fertility. In Egypt, meanwhile, the moon-god Thoth was recognized for other forms of illumination: as patron of science and literature, wisdom and inventions.

Over the years, the moon has been associated with myths and folk tales, some of which attempt to explain its numerous changes in appearance. One story suggests that when the moon wears a shroud of mist, the number of stars one can count in close proximity represents the number of days of rain ahead.

Galileo confirmed that even a mathematician, astronomer, and physicist could be moved to poetic praise and artistic expression by lunar elegance. "It is a most beautiful and delightful sight to behold the body of the moon," he wrote. Then he produced a series of water colors – the world's first maps of the moon – based on his telescope observations in 1610.

In 1980, Provincial Papers decided to produce a calendar as a promotional gift for customers. The moon seemed a logical choice for the theme. After all, moons have long been used as a measure of the seasons. Even today, there are farmers who plant their crops only when the moon is in the right phase. The Mohammedan and Hebrew calendars are still based on the lunar cycle, and our own calendar months have their roots in the lunar cycle even though their lengths have been amended to tie in with the more pragmatic cycle of the sun.

Above: The Moon Goddess *appeared on the calendar cover.*

Below: The Horned Moon, *1980, oil on board, 10 by 10 in. Private collection.*

Facing Page: The Honeymoon, *1980, oil on board, 10 by 10 in. This image reflects the moon's longstanding association with love and romance.*

Page 142: The Gardener, *1980, oil on board, 10 by 10 in. Some of us with green thumbs insist that bulbs should be planted during the waning of the moon. The scarcity of light causes the bulb to send out roots before it sprouts. Private collection.*

Page 143: The Reflection, *1980, oil on board, 10 by 10 in. An old folk tale suggests that if a woman drinks from a pond that holds the reflection of the moon she will become fertile. Private collection.*

Page 144: The Cutting of Hair, *1980. Oil on board, 10 by 10 in. Those who believe that cutting their hair and fingernails saps away*

bodily strength should limit such grooming to when the moon is waxing. Legend has it that the extra strength that accompanies bright moonlight will help to keep personal fatigue to a minimum. Private collection.

Page 145: Witchcraft, *1980, oil on board, 10 by 10 in. The ancients saw the moon as the opponent of the sun, therefore a fitting symbol for the powers of darkness. For witches and other sorcerers the moon was believed to have been the source of their magical powers. The Black Book instructs that they must sit within a protective magic circle when invoking the transfer of power. Private collection.*

Nicholas Jenson was a master engraver at the French mint when word of Gutenberg's achievements with movable type filtered out of Germany. Charles VII, King of France, sent Jenson off to work for Gutenberg and to find out what was going on. But by the time that Jenson returned to France, King Charles had died, and his son, Louis XI, showed little interest in the graphic arts. Jenson moved on to Venice where he produced many fine books and, more importantly, redesigned characters from the old Roman alphabet, many of which have remained essentially unchanged to the present day.

Jenson's pivotal role in printing and publishing encouraged Provincial Papers to name their leading fine paper Jenson Gloss. In 1986, I produced a promotional package for Jenson: a folder and three posters, each printed on a different weight of coated stock. I continued with the historical theme suggested by the name and chose to depict highlights and milestones in the history of the graphic arts, or art in the service of communication.

To research the project, I first gathered together books and publications on the subject, selected and categorized the written and visual information, and finally contacted the various institutions that held copyright and transparencies of the required images.

Projects of this kind, in which commercial content plays a very soft second fiddle behind a chorus of educational information, are rare enough that it's usually easy to solicit the necessary materials. From the Pierpont Morgan Library in New York I borrowed a transparency of a page from the Gutenberg Bible. From the British Library I borrowed transparencies of pages from the Lindisfarne Gospels, one of antiquity's oldest and most beautiful surviving manuscripts. Visual material was also supplied by the Thomas Fischer

Rare Book Library in Toronto and the Centre for Remote Sensing. Other images were reproduced from books, photographed, or in the case of the Book of Kells, were my "artist's interpretations".

Above: The "artist's interpretation" of an ornament from the Book of Kells.

Below: Charlemagne had his own "logo", which was affixed to all royal proclamations.

Facing page: Cover of the folder that held the three Jenson posters.

Page 148: Inside front cover of the Jenson folder.

Page 149: The first poster in the series, highlighted by a page from the Lindisfarne Gospels.

Pages 150 and 151: Details from the Lindisfarne Gospels.

Page 152: Focal point of the second poster was a page from the Gutenberg Bible.

Page 153: Johann Fust was a financial backer of Gutenberg. Before Gutenberg had a chance to pay him back from the earnings on his celebrated Bible, Fust sued and was awarded all of his debtor's equipment, along with the extraordinary invention. This intricate capital B was one of the letters cut and cast for Gutenberg and later used by Fust & Schoeffer, the company Fust founded and turned into the world's first successful printing firm.

Page 154: Detail of a landsat image from the third Jenson poster.

Page 155: The third poster in the series dealt primarily with photography. The main picture demonstrates how digitalized images can be manipulated and merged to dramatic effect.

JENSON

JENSON

Jenson Gloss takes its name from Nicholas Jenson, one of the pivotal figures in the history of the graphic arts. Born in France in the early 15th century, he took up the trade of engraving, and rose to become Master Engraver of the Royal Mint at Tours under Charles VII. When, about mid-century, word reached the French court of a new 'art of printing' emerging in Germany, Charles shrewdly dispatched Jenson to investigate by seeking employment with none other than Gutenberg himself. When Jenson returned to Paris in 1461, Charles had died, and his son Louis XI showed no interest in what Jenson had learned. Determined to be a part of what he knew was an unfolding revolution in the graphic arts, Jenson left Paris for Venice, where he launched his own printing and publishing house. By 1470, he was producing some of Europe's finest books, set completely in typefaces he had designed and cut himself. His work earned him many honours, including the title Count Palatine, granted by Pope Sixtus IV. He died in 1481, having played a leading role in the great transition from the era of rare and limited manuscript books to the still-widening world of modern printing.

Perhaps the greatest testimony to the quality of Jenson's work is the fact that the letterforms he revived and redesigned on classical principles remain essentially unchanged to this day. It was in Jenson's hands that the Roman alphabet was reborn, after centuries of being transformed by the demands of quill pen inscription. Jenson's work gave moveable type technology the faces it needed to fully exploit the new-found power of the press. Even today, computer type-generating programs draw new characters according to principles first established in Jenson's atelier over 500 years ago.

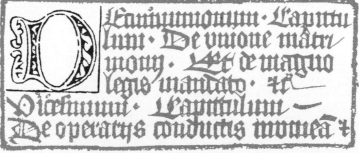

Jenson

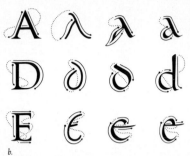

a.

b.

c.

a. The image of St. Mark, woven into an elaborately ornamented title page to his Gospel, is typical of the lavish decoration in the Book of Kells, one of the finest surviving Medieval manuscript books.

b. Smooth hand movements are essential to good writing. In response to the demands of penmanship, the classical geometry of the ancient Roman alphabet was gradually altered to become the thick-and-thin script which Medieval monks inscribed between carefully ruled lines in manuscript books.

c. Heads of birds and other animals frequently appear in ornamented lettering in the Lindisfarne Gospels. These letters (O and P from the word 'opus') appear on the initial page of the Epistle of St. Jerome, whose Latin Vulgate was the version of the Gospels used for this book.

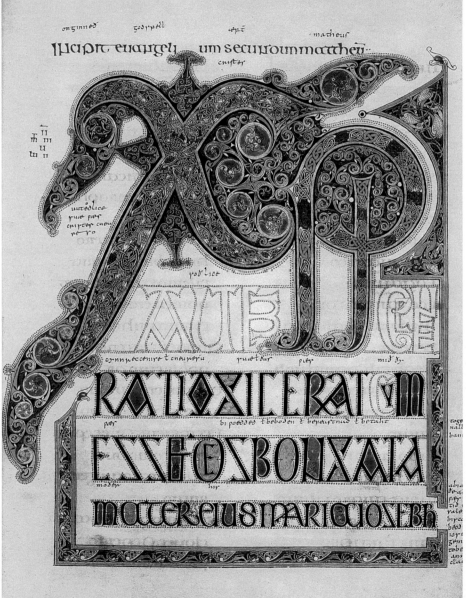

e.

d.

e. Ornate capitals such as this letter Q are common throughout the Book of Kells. Called 'grotesques', these complex initials blend human, animal and fantasy forms into strange and mysterious designs with an overpowering visual richness.

f. The script used in both the Book of Kells and the Lindisfarne Gospels is called insular majuscule. This example, by one of the Book of Kells' three anonymous scribes, is taken from the Gospel of St. Mark.

g. Charlemagne's proclamations in the ninth century carried a Medieval version of what is known as a logotype today, a stylized treatment of combined letterforms creating a visually striking emblem.

f.

d. The Lindisfarne Gospels, one of the oldest and most beautiful of surviving manuscript books, was written and illuminated by a single scribe named Eadfrith, who later became Bishop of the Lindisfarne Church on a tiny island off the northeast coast of England. This initial page from the Gospel of St. Matthew is an outstanding example of the book's intricate, curvilinear ornamentation, painstakingly built up over a geometric framework constructed with compass and ruler. Dozens of exotic pigments, as well as small amounts of gold, were used to colour the decorations.

g.

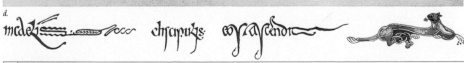

▲ PROVINCIAL
  PAPERS

149

This poster is printed on Jenson Gloss 140M, Provincial Paper's no. 1 grade coated sheet, designed for state-of-the-art reproduction. a., e., f. Artist's Interpretation c., d. Courtesy of The British Library

perc

IENSON

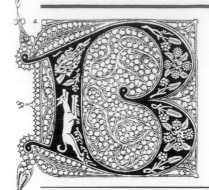

Glos appellatur mariti soror: atq; idem fratris uxor.
Leuir dicitur frater mariti: quasi leuus uir.
Fratris appellantur quasi fratrum inter se uxores.
Amitini fratrum & matris & foeminæ filii.
Patrueles matrum fratrum filii.
Cósobrini ex duabus editi sororibus: de quibus exempla multa sunt in antiquis auctoribus: & maxime in Affranio: & uiris uetutissimis scriptoribus.

NONII MARCELLI PERIPATETICI TIBVRTICENSIS COMPENDIOSA DOCTRINA AD FILIVM DE PROPRIETATE SERMONVM IMPRESSA VENETIIS INDVSTRIA ATQVE IMPENDIO NICOLAI IENSON GALLICI. .M.CCCC.LXXVI.

NOARUS

a. A set of capitals complete with separate decorations was cut and cast for Gutenberg and later used by Fust & Schoiffer in their 1457 psalter, one of the first books – as they proudly noted – to be produced 'without the use of a pen'.

b. Jenson's Roman typeface, cut in about 1470, revived the classic capitals of antiquity and gave the lower case alphabet a cleaner, more elegant look. Both innovations helped adapt letterforms to the new demands of mechanical typography.

c. Albrecht Durer's woodcuts raised this technique to new heights of subtlety and finesse. This one is from his Life of the Virgin Mary (1511), a book which also used an Italian-style typeface of the kind cut earlier by Jenson.

d. Gutenberg's Bible (1455), the first complete book produced from moveable type, started a revolution in the graphic arts, but its pages have a decidedly Medieval look to modern eyes. Its type-style deliberately imitates the hand lettering it replaced, and the printers left plenty of room for rubricators and illuminators to decorate each page by hand in the traditional manner.

Curiosity about the new moveable type technology prompted Charles VII of France to send Nicholas Jenson on a fact-finding mission to Germany. After Charles' death, Jenson went on to Venice to become one of the leading typecutters and printers of his era.

d.

e. Copperplate engraving gave calligraphers a new lease on life at a time when hand-lettering had all but disappeared. Just as the shift from pens to metal type led to changes in the shapes of letterforms, so the practice of hand-engraving letters directly onto plates led to a new kind of flowing, often extravagantly ornate cursive script.

f. Metal engravings supplanted woodcuts both because they reproduce more sophisticated and refined images and because they are more durable on the press. This late 18th century work by Jean-Jacques-François Le Barbier appeared in an edition of the complete works of Jean-Jacques Rousseau.

g. A design diagram of a capital from Geoffroy Troy's Champs Fleury sets out the classical proportions revived by Jenson, among others. These letterforms, dating from well before the time of Christ, remain essentially unaltered today, and are probably the oldest artifacts of Western civilization still in use.

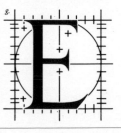

g.

PROVINCIAL PAPERS

This poster is printed on Jenson Gloss 160M, Provincial Papers' no. 1 grade coated sheet, designed for state-of-the-art reproduction.   d. Courtesy of Pierpont Morgan Library

JENSON

a.

a. Botanical detail from an example of photoglyptic gravure.

b, d. The rapid evolution of photography from early monochrome negatives to finely-detailed, full-colour images presented a new challenge to the graphic arts. The half-tone screen process, which etches the image as an array of tiny dots of varying size, provided the required solution.

b.

e. d.

g.

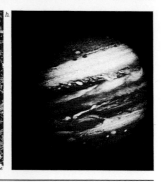

h.

c.

c. A glass window in Lacock Abbey. The oldest known negative, August 1835. The original is violet-toned.

e, f. The four-colour process superimposes a set of four half-tone dot patterns on top of each other, blending magenta, cyan, yellow and black to approximate virtually any hue. Greatly enlarged, these coloured dot patterns resemble the 'pointillist' technique of painters such as Georges Seurat. Nature's own pointillist technique is revealed in an enlarged segment of a butterfly's wing.

f.

k. Eliminating the sawtoothed edges of lines curving across the grid of pixels requires a bit of visual trickery. At very coarse resolution, the pattern on the right appears unintelligible. But with extra grey pixels added, it can be recognized at a distance of about 20 feet as an ampersand. At normal resolution, this technique makes ragged edges invisible to the naked eye.

l. Computer typography uses digital 'bit maps' to store and reproduce the precise shapes of letterforms. To avoid storing complete digital records of every character in hundreds of faces and point sizes, systems are now being developed which reconstruct each character on demand, using only a set of key points stored in memory. Curves between points are computed according to mathematical formulae which are part of the character-generating program.

i.

Digitized images are composed of a very fine grid of picture elements called pixels. An electronic scanner 'reads' each pixel and stores this information as a number in a computer's memory or storage device. Once converted into this digital record, the image can be recalled then processed in many ways to enhance its appearance or the information it contains.

g. Landsat images of earth's surface are made from digital data acquired by electronic scanners aboard orbiting satellites. Combinations of images scanned at different wavelengths create 'false colour' pictures emphasizing particular details.

k.

h. Digital images of Jupiter made by the Voyager space probes were colour-enhanced (exaggerating reds and blues at the expense of greens) to accentuate differences in the types of clouds in the giant gas planet's atmosphere.

i. Electronic colour prepress systems allow digitalized images to be manipulated and merged in many ways previously difficult or impossible to achieve convincingly. By enlarging affected areas and altering them pixel-by-pixel, images from a variety of original sources can be smoothly integrated into a single composition.

j. A different kind of digital processing known as posterization was used to impose a new colour scheme on the clown's face.

j.

l.

R

PROVINCIAL
PAPERS

This poster is printed on Jenson Gloss 200M, Provincial Papers no. 1 grade coated sheet, designed for state-of-the-art reproduction. f. Courtesy of Canadian Centre for Remote Sensing g. Courtesy of NASA

The Making of a Book

My love affair with books began when I was 10 years old, with a leather-bound illustrated volume on the Tannhauser legend. The book, one of a limited edition of 525, was owned by my father, whose taste for rare works always seemed to surpass his ability to afford them. Nevertheless, as a young girl I was captivated by the illustrations of Willy Pogany and, of course, by the legend itself.

Tannhauser is the story of a German knight who had drank long and hard at the well of wretched excess in the court of Venus. One day he saw the light and made a papal pilgrimage to seek redemption, only to be told:

> Sooner this staff on which I lean
> Shall deck itself in tender green
> Than hope of grace shall bloom
> for thee.

The twist to the story is that after Tannhauser left, believing he was doomed for eternity, the holy man's staff did indeed burst into bloom. Messengers were sent to track him down with the news, but by then it was too late.

In 1980, a friend miraculously discovered a duplicate of that book from the same limited edition. I hadn't seen it for years, but as I turned the pages I was stunned to see how much it had influenced my work.

The idea of producing a book of my own is something that I have dreamed of for a long time. I have been approached several times by Canadian publishers with that idea in mind. But, largely because of the diversity of my output as a painter, designer, and illustrator, no one seemed to have a clear idea of what such a book could contain, how and where it might be sold, or whether it could be sold at all!

Then one day in the winter of 1986, it hit me: I would publish the book myself.

My first obstacle was to put aside the worries of friends and colleagues who seemed convinced that I had taken complete leave of my senses. Didn't I know how expensive such a book would be to put together? Didn't I know how precarious today's book publishing business has become, particularly in Canada? Ontario has seen some well-publicized bail-outs by the Provincial Government.

But I believed I knew the "market" for such a book. And I certainly knew the "product" well enough. As I've been producing work to sell other people's goods and services for well over 20 years, it made perfectly good sense that I should be able to produce and sell a book of my own.

But caution has never been an easy thing for me to sweep aside. This may be why I started out with a less ambitious project in mind – something in the order of sixty pages or so. But once I started mapping out the content I realized that I would not get off so lightly.

The first step was to arrange, size, and categorize the images and in pencil sketch form, establish the design, and typographic format. Then, working with photocopies of the sketches, I prepared a dummy that allowed me to get a feeling for the pacing of the book.

The next step was to arrange for the photography of all the paintings, illustrations, and three-dimensional designs. This proved to be easier said than done. Much of the work is in private collections, some in distant cities. In order to achieve fine quality reproduction it was necessary to obtain four-by-five or eight-by-ten transparencies of each image.

Which brings us to the choice of paper. By now you will have already seen my work to promote Provincial Papers' Jenson Gloss to other people. It's an easy product to put your heart into and is widely regarded as the finest coated paper made in Canada today. Mike Catalfamo of Provincial Papers gave me expert advice regarding the paper's special properties. Its smoothness holds the inks up high on the surface of the sheet; this gives the printed areas a natural gloss and brings out the most intricate detail. The brightness of the paper creates strong contrasts between the image and the background and keeps the colors true to the original work. Its opacity prevents the images from showing through from the page behind. And the paper is rugged enough to stand up to the rigors of the binding process, and to what I hope will be years of use from those who buy the book.

The task of getting the work onto pages and turning those pages into a book was made much easier by my choice of collaborators. By bringing these experts together at an early stage in the work we not only avoided unexpected problems, but also allowed everyone on the team to contribute ideas. These ideas significantly enhanced the finished book.

For the color separations I was fortunate enough to work with Ernie Herzig and Hans Lehmkuhl of Herzig Somerville. As anyone in my business could quickly confirm, the quality of the color separations can make or break a book of this kind. Herzig Somerville has a well-earned reputation for marrying advanced technology with old-fashioned personal attention – all for the goal of staying faithful to the original image.

Our printer was Arthurs-Jones of Toronto, one of Canada's foremost lithographers. The company has been in business since 1906 and, particularly over the past 10 years, has produced a good number of high quality art books. I worked with Duncan McGregor and Bob Carter; their expertise and their understanding of the needs of those involved in the other stages of the book helped

immeasurably in making things run smoothly.

Although I have long had a good working knowledge of such areas as paper, color separations, and printing, when it came to the field of book binding I was an absolute rookie. Fortunately, David Friesen and Bob Hamilton of Friesen Printers, were generous with their time and patiently coached me through the intricacies of stitching, choosing end papers, hot stamping, and cloth selection. They introduced me to Mike Davies of Columbia Finishing Mills who gave me a post-graduate course on the fabric and board used in binding. I was given hard-bound mock-ups of the book to judge for size and weight. At last I was able to picture what the finished book would feel like in my hand!

Through the bindery I was also introduced to a distributing company, with whom I concluded an agreement to get the book into stores, removing yet another common deterrent against publishing one's own book.

All that was needed now were the words that would fall between the pictures. I knew that David Parry, a longtime colleague from the early days of Roots, would be able to help me organize my thoughts into some kind of logical order. But I also knew that David had given up almost all of his commercial business and moved to the hills of Northumberland County to write crime fiction. Would he leave the killers and corpses in his word processor long enough to help an old friend? He would, he did, and I'm grateful.

But the most important relationship with any printed work remains the bond between the author and the reader. In reaching this point in the book, you've certainly kept your end of the bargain. I hope you'll agree that I've kept mine.

Design

Heather Cooper Communication
By Design Ltd.
2 Gloucester Street, Suite 302
Toronto, Ontario
Canada M4Y 1L5

Typography

Cooper & Beatty
The Composing Room
401 Wellington Street, West
Toronto, Ontario
Canada M5V 1E8

Typeface: Poppl Pontifex, Berthold System
Technical Notes: A Data Management System
with twin 70 mB hard disc storage, complete
with Berthold's New Software Generation
operating systems was used to provide instant
accessibility and state-of-the-art kerning.

Separations

Herzig Somerville Limited
42 Hollinger Road
Toronto, Ontario
Canada M4B 3G6

Technical Notes: A Crosfield Magnascan 645
Color Scanner was used to produce the color
separations and a Crosfield Studio 830
pagination system was used to assemble the
complete pages electronically.

Paper

Provincial Papers Limited
250 Ferrand Drive, Suite 630
Don Mills, Ontario
Canada M3C 3G8

Quality: The grade of paper used in this book
is manufactured by Provincial Papers at their
Thunder Bay, Ontario mill. It is sold under
the name Jenson Gloss and is widely regarded
as the finest coated printing paper manufactured in Canada today. The weight selected for
this project is 200M.

Pages 56 and 57: Forests (detail), oil on
canvas, 21¼ by 18¼ in. Commissioned in 1986
by the Ministry of Natural Resources.

Page 58: The Paint Box.

Page 59: Self-Portrait.

Printing

Arthurs-Jones Lithographing Ltd.
1060 Tristar Drive
Mississauga, Ontario
Canada L5T 1H9

Technical Notes: The pages of this book were
reproduced as a 200-line screen, using the
four process colors, with two blacks and an
overall varnish. The book was printed on a
six-color, 28" x 40" Heidelberg Speedmaster
with Computerized Print Control (C.P.C.)
I, II and III, and alcohol dampening system.
Lester printing inks and Hoechst N4-100 pre-
sensitized negative plates were utilized.

Binding

Friesen Printers
D.W. Friesen & Sons Ltd.
Box 720, Altona, Manitoba
Canada R0G 0B0

Technical Notes: The printed sheets were
folded on a Stahl T-78 Folder. The signatures
were then sewn on a Mueller-Martini 3210
high speed book sewing machine. A Kolbus
Casing-In machine was used to attach the
hardcover and the end papers to the book
block. The cover fabric is Milbank Vellum,
manufactured by Columbia Finishing Mills.